Stir Fry Cookbook

By Brad Hoskinson

Table of Contents

Kung Pao Chicken

Kung Pao chicken is a popular Chinese dish typically served with steamed rice. The dish is made with chicken, peanuts, and chili peppers and is flavored with soy sauce and sesame oil. Kung Pao chicken is a spicy dish that can be made with varying heat levels, depending on your preference.

PREP TIME 20 minutes | COOK TIME 15 minutes | TOTAL TIME 35 minutes

Ingredients

Chicken

- ✓ 2 lbs boneless skinless chicken thighs or breasts, cut into 1-inch cubes
- ✓ 2 Tbsp cooking oil
- ✓ 3 Tbsp cooking sherry
- ✓ 3 Tbsp soy sauce
- ✓ 3 Tbsp corn starch

Sauce

- ✓ 1cup chicken stock
- ✓ 7 Tbsp soy sauce
- ✓ 3 Tbsp white vinegar
- ✓ 3 Tbsp cooking sherry
- ✓ 3 Tbsp hoisin sauce
- ✓ 3 Tbsp sugar
- ✓ 2 Tbsp corn starch

Stir Fry

- ✓ 5 Tbsp cooking oil divided
- ✓ 3 Tbsp garlic (6-8 cloves)
- ✓ 4 Tbsp ginger
- ✓ 2 red bell pepper
- ✓ 2 green bell pepper
- ✓ 11 dried chilies
- ✓ 5 green onions cut into 1-inch pieces
- ✓ 1 cup roasted peanuts
- ✓ 3 tsp sesame oil

Instructions

1. First, mix all chicken ingredients, and set them aside.
2. While chicken marinates, mix sauce and dice vegetables.
3. Heat a large skillet or wok over high heat. Add 3 tbs cooking oil, then fry chicken for 6 minutes, stirring occasionally. Once it begins to brown, remove it from the pan and set it aside.
4. Add remaining cooking oil, ginger, garlic, chili, pepper, and bell peppers. Fry for 1 minute, stirring frequently.
5. Add sauce and bring to boil. Once it thickens, add chicken and mix everything nicely for about 3 minutes.
6. Add peanuts, green onions, and sesame oil, and simmer for about 3 minutes.
7. Serve with rice. Enjoy!

Mongolian Beef

Mongolian beef is a dish that is popular in Chinese cuisine. The dish is made by stir-frying beef with vegetables and is typically served with rice or noodles. Mongolian beef is a variation of the traditional dish of beef and broccoli.

PREP TIME 20 minutes | COOK TIME 20 minutes | TOTAL TIME 40 minutes

Ingredients

Stir Fry

- ✓ 2 lbs flank steak
- ✓ 1 onion
- ✓ 6 green onions
- ✓ 6 cloves garlic
- ✓ 2 Tbsp chopped ginger
- ✓ 5 dried red chilis
- ✓ 5 Tbsp oil, divided

Marinade

- ✓ 2 Tbsp soy sauce
- ✓ 3 Tbsp Chinese wine (optional)
- ✓ 7 tsp corn starch or 1 tsp xanthan gum
- ✓ 2 tsp baking soda

Sauce

- ✓ 1 cup soy sauce or tamari sauce
- ✓ 1 cup chicken stock
- ✓ 3/4 cup Chinese wine (optional)
- ✓ 6 Tbsp brown sugar (see note 1 for keto options)
- ✓ 2 Tbsp corn starch or 1 tsp xanthan gum
- ✓ 3 Tbsp water

Instructions

Stir Fry Method

1. Thinly slice beef at an angle, about 3/8 of an inch. Mix with marinade ingredients in a bowl. Add in beef strips and mix well.
2. Chop onions and green onions, separating white and green portions of green onions. Finely chop ginger and garlic. Cut dried red chilis into strips.
3. Mix the first four sauce ingredients. Separately, mix water and corn starch until well blended.
4. Heat 3 Tbsp oil in the wok over medium-high heat. Add meat strips and sear for about 5 minutes per side. Remove and spread on a plate.
5. Heat remaining oil to pan and add onion and white portion of green onions. Stir and cook until slightly softened.
6. Add ginger, garlic, and red chili strips, stir. Add soy sauce, wine, brown sugar, and stock. Add corn starch mixture and stir well. Let simmer until sauce begins to thicken.
7. Stir in meat and green portions of green onions.
8. Serve hot with your favorite rice.

Crock Pot Method

1. Thinly slice beef at an angle, about 3/8 of an inch. Mix with marinade ingredients in a bowl. Add in beef strips and mix well.
2. Chop onions and green onions, separating white and green portions of green onions. Finely chop ginger and garlic. Cut dried red chilis into strips.
3. Mix all sauce ingredients except the green portions of the green onions.
4. Add all ingredients (holding aside the green portion of green onions) to the crock pot.
5. Cover and cook on high for 4 hours or low for 6 hours.
6. Garnish with reserved green onions and serve.

Instant Pot Method

1. Thinly slice beef at an angle, about 3/8 of an inch. Mix with marinade ingredients in a bowl. Add in beef strips and mix well.

2. Chop onions and green onions, separating white and green portions of green onions. Finely chop ginger and garlic. Cut dried red chilis into strips.
3. Mix all sauce ingredients except the green portions of the green onions.
4. Turn your Instant Pot to Saute mode and add in oil. Once hot, add marinated beef and cook 5 minutes to get it a little browned up.
5. Add in your sauce and mix everything well. Close the lid and pressure cook on High pressure for 15 minutes.
6. Allow pressure to naturally release for 15 minutes before opening the lid. Garnish with green onions and serve.

Hunan Shrimp

Hunan shrimp is a popular dish in the Hunan Province of China. The dish consists of shrimp that is cooked in a spicy sauce. The sauce is made with chili peppers, garlic, and soy sauce. Hunan shrimp is a popular dish in China because it is flavorful and spicy.

PREP TIME 15 minutes | COOK TIME 20 minutes | TOTAL TIME 35 minutes

Ingredients

Stir Fry

- ✓ 2 lbs shrimp
- ✓ 2 Tbsp cornstarch
- ✓ 2 cups green beans, chopped
- ✓ 1 green bell pepper, chopped
- ✓ 1 red bell pepper, chopped
- ✓ 1 yellow bell pepper, chopped
- ✓ 1 orange bell pepper, chopped
- ✓ 7 green onions or scallions, chopped
- ✓ 6 garlic cloves, finely chopped
- ✓ 2 Tbsp ginger, finely chopped
- ✓ 1 tsp salt
- ✓ 2 tsp pepper
- ✓ 4 Tbsp oil

Hunan sauce

- ✓ 6 tsp sambal oelek chili paste
- ✓ 3 Tbsp oyster sauce
- ✓ 2 Tbsp soy sauce
- ✓ 2 Tbsp rice or white vinegar
- ✓ 3 Tbsp rice wine
- ✓ 4 Tbsp tomato ketchup
- ✓ 2 tsp sugar

Instructions

1. Clean the shrimp (we kept the tail on) and marinate it with salt, pepper, and cornstarch while you prep the rest of the ingredients.

2. Mix all the ingredients for Hunan sauce in a bowl.
3. Dice all bell peppers, and cut the green beans and scallions into inch-long pieces. Keep the green and white parts of the scallion separate.
4. Heat 3 Tbsp oil in a wok over medium-high heat. Add shrimp and sear for a couple of minutes until they get curled up and turn pink. Plate them out and set them aside. Don't overcook, as they will continue to cook in the Hunan sauce later.
5. Add remaining oil and turn the heat to high. Add in green beans. Stir and cook for a couple of minutes till they get a little soft. Stir in bell peppers, white parts of scallions, ginger, and garlic. Stir fry for 7 minutes, then mix in the prepared Hunan sauce. Add 3/4 to 1 cup of water along with shrimp and stir fry for another 5 minutes. Garnish it with green parts of scallions.
6. Serve it piping hot over your favorite steamed rice.

Teriyaki Shrimp Stir Fry

This quick and easy shrimp stir fry is perfect for a weeknight meal. The shrimp are cooked in a delicious teriyaki sauce and served with a simple vegetable stir fry. You can have this dish on the table in under 30 minutes!

Prep Time 15 minutes | Cook Time 15 minutes | Total Time 30 minutes

Ingredients

For the stir fry:

- ✓ 2 lbs large shrimp peeled and deveined
- ✓ 4 cups of mixed vegetables. I used snow peas and sliced bell peppers
- ✓ salt and pepper to taste
- ✓ 2 tablespoons vegetable oil
- ✓ Optional garnishes: sliced green onions and sesame seeds

For the sauce:

- ✓ 3/4 cup soy sauce
- ✓ 1 cup water
- ✓ 4 tablespoons brown sugar
- ✓ 3 teaspoons minced garlic
- ✓ 3 teaspoons minced ginger
- ✓ 2 tablespoons of honey
- ✓ 2 teaspoons toasted sesame oil
- ✓ 2 tablespoons + 1 teaspoon cornstarch

Instructions

1. For the sauce: Place the soy sauce, water, brown sugar, garlic, ginger, honey, and sesame oil in a small pot over medium-high heat.
2. Stir until sugar is dissolved, about 5 minutes. Turn up the heat to high and bring it to a boil.
3. Mix the cornstarch with 3 tablespoons of cold water until dissolved. Add the cornstarch mixture to the sauce and boil for 3 minutes or until the sauce has thickened. Set sauce aside.

4. For the stir fry: Heat 1 teaspoon vegetable oil in a large pan over medium-high heat. Add the vegetables and season with salt and pepper to taste.
5. Cook for 6 minutes or until vegetables has started to brown and soften. Add 3 tablespoons of water and cook until water has evaporated. When your vegetables are crisp-tender, remove them from the pan and set them aside.
6. Wipe out the pan. Heat the remaining 3 teaspoons of oil in the pan over high heat.
7. Place the shrimp in the pan and season generously with salt and pepper. Cook for 5 minutes or until just cooked through (shrimp should be pink and opaque).
8. Add the vegetables back to the pan. Pour the sauce over the top and cook for 3 minutes over medium-high heat until warm.
9. Garnish with sesame seeds and sliced green onions if desired.

Korean Ground Beef Bowl

Ground beef is a staple in most households and can be used in many different dishes. This recipe for a Korean ground beef bowl is easy to make and is sure to be a family favorite. The beef is cooked with onions, garlic, and ginger, then served over rice with various toppings, including kimchi, green onions, and sesame seeds.

PREP TIME 10 minutes | COOK TIME 20 minutes | TOTAL TIME 30 minutes

Ingredients

- ✓ 2 lbs ground beef
- ✓ 3/4 cup soy sauce
- ✓ 3/4 cup brown sugar
- ✓ 4 chopped green onions
- ✓ 3 Tbsp chopped garlic
- ✓ 2 Tbsp chopped ginger
- ✓ 3 Tbsp chopped cilantro
- ✓ 1.5 tsp red chili flakes
- ✓ 3 tsp sesame oil
- ✓ 2 Tbsp sesame seeds

Instructions

1. Chop ginger, garlic, onions, and cilantro.
2. Whisk soy sauce, brown sugar, red chili flakes, and sesame oil in a bowl, and set aside.
3. In a large skillet or wok, sauté ground beef until no longer pink, 7 minutes. Stir in garlic, ginger, and half of the green onions. Cook for 2 minutes.
4. Stir in sauce mixture, and simmer for 7 minutes until sauce is slightly reduced.
5. Stir in the remaining green onions, and garnish with sesame seeds and cilantro.
6. Serve in a bowl with cooked white rice and your choice of veggies.

Thai Basil Chicken

One of my favorite Thai dishes is basil chicken. It is a stir-fry dish with chicken, onions, and bell peppers in a savory sauce made with fish sauce, soy sauce, garlic, and sugar. I like to serve it over steamed rice.

PREP TIME 10 minutes | COOK TIME 20 minutes | TOTAL TIME 30 minutes

Ingredients

- ✓ 2 lbs ground chicken
- ✓ 2 cup basil
- ✓ 13-15 cloves of garlic
- ✓ 9-10 red bird chilis
- ✓ 4 Tbsp soy sauce
- ✓ 4 Tbsp oyster sauce
- ✓ 2 Tbsp fish sauce
- ✓ 2 tsp sugar
- ✓ 4 Tbsp vegetable oil
- ✓ 5 eggs

Instructions

Thai Basil Chicken

1. Crush chilis and peeled garlic into a paste.
2. Heat oil in a wok over high heat. Add the chili-garlic paste and stir for 25 seconds.
3. Add chicken and stir for 9-10 minutes, or until chicken is thoroughly cooked.
4. Add sugar and sauces, stir until well mixed.
5. Fold in basil. Remove from heat immediately so the basil doesn't overcook.

Eggs

1. Fill the frying pan with 3/4 inch of oil. Get nice and hot.
2. Drop in eggs. Fry until edges are nice and crispy, spooning hot oil over eggs to cook the top.
3. Cook until the desired doneness.

Hawaiian Pineapple Fried Rice

Hawaiian Pineapple Fried Rice is a delicious, easy-to-make dish that is perfect for any occasion. This dish is made with white rice, diced pineapple, soy sauce, and green onions. It can be served as a main course or as a side dish.

PREP TIME 15 minutes | COOK TIME 15 minutes | TOTAL TIME 30 minutes

Ingredients

- ✓ 5 cups cooked rice (basmati)
- ✓ 3 cups chopped cooked ham
- ✓ 1 cup carrot, chopped
- ✓ 1 cup peas
- ✓ 1 cup onions
- ✓ 1 red bell pepper
- ✓ 1 green bell pepper
- ✓ 4 scallions, chopped
- ✓ 2 Tbsp chopped ginger
- ✓ 4 garlic cloves, chopped
- ✓ 2 cups chopped pineapple
- ✓ 4 eggs
- ✓ 5 Tbsp soy sauce
- ✓ 3 tsp oyster sauce
- ✓ 1 tsp sesame oil
- ✓ 5 Tbsp cooking oil, divided

Instructions

1. Chop ham and all vegetables, along with garlic and ginger. Whisk eggs in a bowl.
2. Heat wok or large skillet over large heat. Add 4 Tbsp cooking oil. Once hot, add onion, white parts of green onions, and peppers. Sauté 1 minute.
3. Add carrots, ginger, garlic, and ham. Stir fry for 4-5 minutes. Add peas, stir and move everything to one side of the pan.
4. Add remaining 2 Tbsp cooking oil to empty side of pan. Once hot, add whisked eggs and scramble until cooked but still soft. Mix all ingredients in a pan together.

5. Add rice along with soy sauce, oyster sauce, and sesame oil. Mix well and stir fry for 3-4 minutes.
6. Add pineapple, mix well and remove from heat. Serve and garnish with a green portion of green onions.

Healthy Chicken Ramen Stir Fry

Ramen noodles are a college student's best friend. They are cheap, filling, and can be made in minutes. But what about when you're tired of eating them plain? This healthy chicken ramen stir fry is the perfect way to change up your usual routine and add some new flavors to your meal. The recipe is simple to follow and can be easily adapted to include your favorite vegetables.

PREP TIME 10 minutes | COOK TIME 15 minutes | TOTAL TIME 20 minutes

Ingredients

- ✓ 2 large chicken breasts
- ✓ 3 packets of ramen noodles (minus flavoring packets)
- ✓ 2 small onions
- ✓ 2 red bell pepper
- ✓ 2 green bell pepper
- ✓ 8-9 mushrooms
- ✓ 12-15 baby carrots
- ✓ 4 scallions
- ✓ 5 garlic cloves
- ✓ 2 Tbsp chopped ginger
- ✓ 4 Tbsp cooking oil
- ✓ 4 Tbsp soy sauce
- ✓ 3 Tbsp Hoisin sauce
- ✓ 3 Tbsp oyster sauce
- ✓ 3 Tbsp sweet chili sauce
- ✓ 2 cups water

Instructions

1. First, get everything prepped. Finely chop ginger and garlic, slice mushrooms, onions and peppers, and matchstick carrots. Cut scallions into one-inch slices and keep green and white portions separate. Also, mix all of your sauce ingredients, soy, Hoising, oyster, and sweet chili, together in a bowl. First butterfly chicken breast, then cut into thin strips.

2. Get a wok or large skillet hot over high heat. Once it is sizzling hot, add oil, chopped onions, and white portions of scallions. Sauté one minute, then add chicken. Stirring frequently, cook until the pink color has left chicken, 5-6 minutes.
3. Add ginger and garlic and toss together for about one minute. Then add carrots, peppers, and mushrooms. Stir fry for 5-6 minutes. Add sauces, and mix well.
4. Make well by moving stir fry ingredients to the perimeter of the wok. Add water to the well. Let heat for about a minute; it should start simmering.
5. Add ramen to well, and cook for one minute. Flip and cook an additional minute.
6. Separate the noodles and mix well with other ingredients.
7. Serve hot and garnish with the remaining part of the scallions.

Beef and Broccoli Recipe

The following beef and broccoli recipe is a great way to enjoy this classic dish. The beef is cooked with onions and garlic, then simmered in a savory broth until tender. Fresh broccoli is added at the end, ensuring that it retains its crispness. This dish is perfect for a quick and easy weeknight meal.

Prep Time: 20 minutes Cook Time: 15 minutes Total Time: 35 minutes

Ingredients

- ✓ Beef and Broccoli Ingredients:
- ✓ 2 lb flank steak, very thinly sliced into bite-sized strips
- ✓ 3 Tbsp olive oil (or vegetable oil), divided
- ✓ 2 lb broccoli (cut into 6 cups of florets)
- ✓ 3 tsp sesame seeds, optional garnish
- ✓ Stir Fry Sauce Ingredients:
- ✓ 2 tsp fresh ginger, grated (loosely packed)
- ✓ 3 tsp garlic, grated (from 3 cloves)
- ✓ 1 cup hot water
- ✓ 7 Tbsp low sodium soy sauce (or GF Tamari)
- ✓ 4 Tbsp packed light brown sugar
- ✓ 2 Tbsp corn starch
- ✓ 3/4 tsp black pepper
- ✓ 3 Tbsp sesame oil

Instructions

1. Prep: Start cooking white rice first, so it's ready when the stir fry is done. Cover and freeze steak for 30 minutes for easier slicing.
2. Combine all stir fry sauce ingredients in a bowl, stir well to dissolve the sugar, and set aside.
3. Place a large skillet over medium heat and add 2 Tbsp oil. Add broccoli florets and sauté for 4-5 minutes, partially covered with a lid, stirring or tossing several times until broccoli is bright green and crisp-tender, then remove from the pan. **Tip:** If you prefer softer broccoli, add 3 Tbsp water before covering with the lid and it will steam cook the broccoli.

4. Increase heat to high heat and add 2 Tbsp oil. Add beef in a single layer and sauté for 2 minutes per side or just until cooked through. Quickly pull out a piece to test for doneness.
5. Add the sauce, reduce heat to medium/low and simmer for 4-5 minutes. It will thicken. Add broccoli and stir to combine. Stir in 2-3 Tbsp water to thin the sauce if desired. Serve over white rice.

Orange Garlic Shrimp

Garlic shrimp is a popular dish that can be made with shrimp, garlic, butter, and olive oil. The dish can also be made with other ingredients, such as orange juice. The orange juice in this recipe gives the shrimp a sweet and tangy flavor that makes the dish taste great. Garlic shrimp can be served as an appetizer or a main course.

Servings: 5 | Prep 25 minutes | Cook 15 minutes

Ingredients

Sauce

- ✓ 1 cup fresh orange juice
- ✓ 2 tsp orange zest
- ✓ 2/3 cup unsalted or low-sodium chicken broth
- ✓ 3 Tbsp soy sauce
- ✓ 4 Tbsp honey
- ✓ 3 tsp lemon juice or rice wine vinegar
- ✓ 3/8 tsp red pepper flakes (optional)
- ✓ 3 tsp cornstarch

Shrimp

- ✓ 2 lb large shrimp, peeled and deveined
- ✓ Salt and pepper to taste
- ✓ 1 tsp sesame oil
- ✓ 2 Tbsp vegetable oil
- ✓ 1 cup chopped bell peppers, cut into 1/2-inch pieces
- ✓ 2 cups (8 oz) sugar snap peas
- ✓ 5 cloves garlic, minced (2 Tbsp)
- ✓ 3 tsp peeled and minced fresh ginger
- ✓ 3 Tbsp sliced green onions
- ✓ 1 tsp sesame seeds
- ✓ 3/4 cup cilantro leaves

Instructions

1. To make the sauce, in a medium size bowl, whisk together orange juice, orange zest, chicken broth, soy sauce, honey, lemon juice, red pepper flakes, and cornstarch. Set aside.
2. Pat the shrimp dry with paper towels to remove as much moisture as possible.
3. In a medium bowl, toss shrimp with salt and pepper (about 3/4 tsp of each) and sesame oil.
4. Heat a wok or 12-inch skillet over high heat. Add the oil and heat just until it's beginning to smoke, then add the shrimp to the pan in a single layer and cook for 2 minutes.
5. Flip shrimp to the opposite side and cook until about 2 minutes longer pink. Transfer cooked shrimp to a clean plate.
6. Add the bell peppers and sugar snap peas to the wok in a single layer, and allow to cook for 1 minute without moving. Stir the vegetables and cook until lightly browned and crisp, about 30 seconds.
7. Add the garlic and ginger to the pan and stir fry for 35 seconds.
8. Whisk the orange sauce, then gradually add it to the side of the pan; stir the sauce continuously as it gathers on the bottom of the pan.
9. Allow the sauce to boil, constantly stirring, until the sauce has thickened, about 2 - 3 minutes.
10. Add the shrimp to the pan and allow it to warm for about 30 seconds. Season with more salt and pepper to taste if needed.
11. Garnish with green onions, sesame seeds, and cilantro.
12. Recipe source: recipe from Jessica Gavin's cookbook, Easy Culinary Science for Better Cooking

Cashew Chicken Meal Prep Bowls

These Cashew Chicken Meal Prep Bowls are a healthy and delicious way to start your week on the right foot! The chicken is marinated in a simple cashew sauce, then baked until perfectly tender. Served alongside some cooked rice and roasted broccoli, this meal is healthy, easy to make, and downright delicious.

Prep Time 20 mins | Cook Time 20 mins | Total Time 40 mins

Ingredients

- ✓ 2 lb chicken breasts, diced into 1-inch cubes
- ✓ 2 tbsp cornstarch
- ✓ Salt & pepper to taste
- ✓ 2 tbsp sesame oil
- ✓ 2 cup mushrooms, sliced in half
- ✓ 2 carrots, chopped
- ✓ 2 yellow onions, chopped
- ✓ 2 green peppers, chopped
- ✓ 2 red peppers, chopped
- ✓ 1 cup cashews
- ✓ Stir fry sauce
- ✓ 4 tbsp low-sodium soy sauce or Tamari
- ✓ 3 tbsp honey
- ✓ 5 cloves garlic, minced

Instructions

1. In a large bowl, season chicken with salt & pepper then tosses with cornstarch. Meanwhile, mix the stir fry sauce ingredients in a small bowl and set aside.
2. Heat oil in a large skillet or wok over med-high heat. Add carrots and mushrooms to skillet, cooking for 7 minutes until carrots soften and mushrooms release juices. Add chicken and saute for another 5 minutes until browned, stirring often.
3. Add onion, green pepper, and red pepper to the skillet, sauteeing another 3-5 minutes, then add sauce, cooking for 3-5 more minutes until sauce thickens.
4. Stir in cashews, then remove from heat. Serve garnished with sesame seeds (optional), and enjoy!

Sizzlin' Spicy Szechuan Stir-Fry

One of the many things I love about Chinese cuisine is the diversity of flavors that can be found in its many regional cuisines. Szechuan cuisine is no exception and is famous for its spicy dishes. This Szechuan stir-fry is a perfect example of the flavors you can find in Szechuan cooking. The dish is made with a mixture of chicken, shrimp, and vegetables cooked in a spicy Szechuan sauce.

prep time: 15 MINUTES cook time: 15 MINUTES total time: 30 MINUTES

Ingredients

- ✓ 3 tablespoons avocado oil (or other high-heat oil), divided
- ✓ 2 pounds flank steak, thinly sliced
- ✓ 2 medium white onions, peeled and thinly sliced
- ✓ 2 large red bell pepper, cored and thinly sliced
- ✓ 5 cloves garlic, peeled and thinly sliced
- ✓ 2 batch Szechuan Sauce
- ✓ optional toppings: thinly-sliced green onions, toasted sesame seeds, extra crushed red pepper flakes

Instructions

1. Heat 1 tablespoon oil in a wok or large sauté pan over high heat.
2. Add steak and sauté for 6-7 minutes, occasionally tossing, until cooked. Transfer steak to a clean plate and set aside.
3. Add the remaining 2 tablespoons of oil to the pan, along with the onion and bell pepper. Sauté for 4-5 minutes, occasionally tossing, until cooked by still slightly crispy. (I don't like my veggies to be too soft in a stir-fry.) Add garlic and sauté for 1 more minute, or until fragrant.
4. Reduce heat to medium. Add the steak and Szechuan sauce to the veggies, and toss to combine for about 35 seconds, or until the sauce thickens.
5. Remove from heat and serve immediately over rice or noodles, sprinkled with your desired toppings.

Sweet and Sour Pork

One of the most popular dishes in Chinese cuisine is sweet and sour pork. This dish combines crispy fried pork strips in a sweet and sour sauce. The sauce is usually vinegar, sugar, ketchup, and soy sauce. Some variations also include pineapple or other fruit. Sweet and sour pork is a favorite dish among people of all ages and can be served as a main course or appetizer.

Prep Time 20 mins | Cook Time 25 mins | Total Time 45 mins

Ingredients

Sweet and Sour Sauce

- ✓ 1 cup honey
- ✓ 7 tablespoons rice vinegar
- ✓ 5 teaspoons soy sauce
- ✓ 4 tablespoons tomato paste
- ✓ 2 tablespoons cornstarch
- ✓ 3 tablespoons water

Pork

- ✓ 2 pounds of pork tenderloin cut into 1-inch cubes
- ✓ 2 teaspoons kosher salt divided
- ✓ 1 teaspoon black pepper divided
- ✓ 1 cup all-purpose flour
- ✓ 1 cup cornstarch
- ✓ 3 large eggs
- ✓ 3 cups plus 1 tablespoon vegetable oil for frying
- ✓ 2 tablespoons minced garlic
- ✓ 2 cups chopped white onions 3/4-inch sized pieces
- ✓ 2 cups chopped red bell pepper 3/4-inch sized pieces
- ✓ 2 cups chopped green bell pepper 3/4-inch sized pieces
- ✓ 2 cups pineapple chunks 3/4-inch sized pieces
- ✓ 3 tablespoons sliced green onion
- ✓ 1 teaspoon sesame seeds

Instructions

1. In a medium-sized bowl, combine sweet and sour sauce ingredients, honey, rice vinegar, soy sauce, and tomato paste. Set aside.
2. In a small bowl, combine the cornstarch and water.
3. Season pork with 1 teaspoon salt and 3/4 teaspoon pepper.
4. In a shallow dish, mix together flour and 1 cup of cornstarch.
5. In a separate shallow dish, add eggs and whisk.
6. Batter each piece of pork by coating it with the flour mixture, then dip in the whisked egg, then a final coat in the flour mixture.
7. Heat 3 cups of oil over medium-high heat in a wok or medium-sized pan. Once the oil reaches 370°F (197°C), work in 3 to 5 batches, adding the battered pork and frying until golden brown and the pork is cooked through, about 7 to 9 minutes.
8. Transfer pork to a sheet pan and drain on paper towels. Fry the next batch.
9. Discard the oil from the wok and carefully wipe the inside of the pan with paper towels to clean.
10. Heat a wok over medium-high heat and add 2 tablespoons of oil.
11. Once the oil is hot, add the garlic and onions, and stir-fry for 30 seconds.
12. Add in the red and green bell peppers, and stir-fry for 1 minute.
13. Add in the pineapple and stir-fry for 1 minute.
14. Add in the pork and the sweet and sour sauce, stir to combine and allow the sauce to come to a boil.
15. Stir the cornstarch slurry and then add it to the pan, constantly stirring until the sauce thickens, 65 seconds. Mix the ingredients with the sauce to coat the pork.
16. Garnish the sweet and sour pork with green onions and sesame seeds and serve over rice.

Pepper Steak Stir Fry

This dish is a quick and easy way to get a delicious, nutrient-rich meal on the table. The steak is seared in a hot pan until browned, then removed and set aside. The vegetables are then added to the pan and cooked until tender. The steak is then returned to the pan and everything is cooked through. The result is a flavorful, healthy stir fry that can be served with rice or noodles.

Prep Time 15 minutes | Cook Time 25 minutes | Total Time 40 minutes

Ingredients

- ✓ 2 tablespoons vegetable oil divided use
- ✓ 2 red bell peppers were cored, seeded and cut into strips
- ✓ 2 green bell peppers were cored, seeded and cut into strips
- ✓ 2 pounds flank steak thinly sliced
- ✓ 3 teaspoons minced garlic
- ✓ 2 teaspoons minced ginger
- ✓ salt and pepper to taste
- ✓ 3/4 cup soy sauce
- ✓ 2 tablespoons sugar
- ✓ 2 tablespoons cornstarch

Instructions

1. Heat 1 teaspoon vegetable oil over medium-high heat in a large pan.
2. Add the peppers and cook for 5 minutes or until just tender. Remove the peppers from the pan and place them on a plate.
3. Add the remaining oil to the pan. Season the flank steak with salt and pepper to taste.
4. Increase heat to high. Add the steak to the pan and cook for 7 minutes or until lightly browned.
5. Add the garlic and ginger, then cook for 35 seconds.
6. Place the peppers back in the pan with the steak.
7. Whisk together the soy sauce, sugar, 3/4 cup water, and cornstarch in a small bowl.
8. Pour the sauce over the steak mixture and bring to a simmer. Cook for 5 minutes or until sauce has just thickened, then serve.

Pad Thai (with Chicken or Shrimp)

Pad Thai is a popular Thai dish usually made with chicken or shrimp. It is a stir-fried dish with rice noodles, bean sprouts, eggs, and peanuts. The dish is typically served with a sweet and sour sauce.

Prep 20 minutes | Cook 25 minutes

Ingredients

- ✓ 15 oz Thai rice noodles
- ✓ 2 lb boneless skinless chicken breasts, sliced into small strips, or 2 lb extra large shrimp, peeled and deveined
- ✓ 3 Tbsp vegetable oil
- ✓ 3/4 cup packed dark-brown sugar
- ✓ 3/4 cup soy sauce
- ✓ 3 Tbsp rice vinegar
- ✓ 2 Tbsp lime juice
- ✓ 2 Tbsp fish sauce
- ✓ 2 red bell pepper, sliced into thin strips and strips halved
- ✓ 2 cups matchstick carrots
- ✓ 3 cloves garlic
- ✓ 6 green onions, whites minced, greens sliced into 1-inch pieces
- ✓ 3 cups bean sprouts
- ✓ 4 large eggs
- ✓ 1cup unsalted peanuts, chopped
- ✓ 2/3 cup cilantro, chopped
- ✓ Red pepper flakes and sesame seeds (optional)

Instructions

1. Prepare rice noodles according to the directions listed on the package. In a mixing bowl, whisk together brown sugar, soy sauce, rice vinegar, lime juice, and fish sauce, and set aside.
2. While noodles are cooking, heat oil in a wok or a 12-inch deep saute pan set over medium-high heat. Add chicken and saute until cooked through about 6 minutes. If using shrimp, cook about 2 minutes per side or until opaque.
3. Transfer to a plate, leaving oil in a pan. Add bell pepper and carrots, saute for 2 - 3 minutes, then add garlic, green onions, and bean sprouts; saute 1 minute longer.

4. Push veggies to the edges of the pan and crack eggs into the center. Cook and scramble until eggs have cooked through. Add in chicken, noodles, and sauce, toss everything together, and cook for 2 - 3 minutes.
5. Serve warmly topped with cilantro, peanuts, optional red pepper flakes, and sesame seeds.

Ground Turkey Stir Fry

Ground turkey is a popular choice for a healthy and affordable meal. This stir fry is easy to make and can be tailored to your liking. Start by heating a tablespoon of oil in a wok or large skillet over medium-high heat. Add the onion, bell pepper, and celery and cook until the vegetables are soft, about 5 minutes. Add the ground turkey and cook until browned, about 5 minutes more.

Prep Time 20 mins | Cook Time 20 mins | Total Time 40 mins

Ingredients

- ✓ 2 tbsp olive or sesame oil
- ✓ 2 yellow onions, sliced
- ✓ 2 lb ground turkey
- ✓ 2 pinch salt
- ✓ 2 carrots, grated
- ✓ 2 red peppers, sliced
- ✓ 2 cups chopped red cabbage
- ✓ 5 green onions, sliced
- ✓ Stir fry sauce
- ✓ 3 tbsp low sodium soy sauce
- ✓ 2 tbsp honey
- ✓ 5 cloves garlic, minced
- ✓ 2 tbsp fresh minced ginger
- ✓ 2 tsp sriracha or chili garlic sauce

Instructions

1. Mix ingredients for the sauce together.
2. Heat oil over med-high heat, then adds onions, sauteing for 3 minutes until softened. Add ground turkey, breaking up with a wooden spoon. Add a pinch of salt to season the meat, then saute until lightly browned, about 7 minutes.
3. Add carrot, bell pepper, and cabbage, sauteeing for 5-7 minutes until softened. Add sauce, then cook another 3-5 minutes until well combined and sauce thickens slightly. Remove from heat and stir in green onions. Serve and enjoy!
4. Storing and reheating: Leftovers will last up to 7 days in the fridge. Store individual portions in glass bowls and reheat for 3-5 minutes

in the microwave, or saute on the stovetop for 3-5 minutes until heated.

Mostly Veggie Steak Stir Fry

This Mostly Veggie Steak Stir Fry is a delicious and healthy way to enjoy your steak! The vegetables add a great flavor and nutrition to the dish without adding too many calories. You can customize the stir fry to include your favorite vegetables.

Prep Time 20 minutes | Cook Time 25 minutes | Total Time 45 minutes

Ingredients

- ✓ 2 lb steak (sirloin, skirt, or flank) thinly sliced into ¼" strips against the grain
- ✓ 3 tbsp olive oil divided
- ✓ 3 cloves garlic minced
- ✓ 3 medium carrots peeled and thinly sliced
- ✓ 1 lb asparagus ends trimmed, sliced into 1" pieces
- ✓ 2 red bell pepper cut into thin strips
- ✓ 2 yellow bell pepper cut into thin strips
- ✓ 7 oz snap peas
- ✓ 3 tbsp sesame seeds
- ✓ 2 tsp sea or kosher salt
- ✓ 2 tsp cracked black pepper
- ✓ Stir Fry Sauce
- ✓ 3/4 c coconut aminos
- ✓ 3 tbsp rice vinegar
- ✓ 3 tbsp fresh orange juice
- ✓ 3 tbsp honey
- ✓ 2 tbsp cornstarch or arrowroot powder
- ✓ 3 tsp sesame oil

Instructions

1. Place the steak in the freezer for 35 minutes. Remove from the freezer and slice thinly against the grain, 1/8" – 1/4" thick. While the steak is freezing, prepare the vegetables and stir fry sauce.
2. Combine all stir fry sauce ingredients in a bowl. Whisk until combined and set aside.

3. Heat a 14" cast iron skillet over medium heat. Add half the olive oil. Add half the steak to the skillet, season with salt and pepper, and stir fry until charred and medium rare, 5 minutes. Remove the steak with tongs, set aside onto a plate, and repeat with the remaining steak strips. Remove all steak from the skillet once browned.
4. Add the second tablespoon of olive oil to the skillet and allow to heat until shimmering. Add the garlic and saute for 1 minute. Add the carrots and asparagus and saute for 3 minutes, stirring frequently. Add the bell pepper and snap peas, toss with the asparagus and carrots, and stir fry all vegetables for an additional 5 minutes. Be sure to stir and toss frequently.
5. Add the steak back to the skillet and stir-fried sauce (give it another whisk before pouring in if the cornstarch/arrowroot has settled to the bottom). Stir fry, frequently stirring, until the sauce thickens and the vegetables are bite tender, 5 minutes.
6. Remove from heat, stir in the sesame seeds, and serve immediately. Leftovers can be stored in the fridge in a tightly sealed container for up to 5 days.

Beef Chow Fun (Beef & Noodle Stir Fry)

This dish is a popular one in Chinese cuisine. It is a stir-fry of beef and noodles, typically made with flank steak and rice noodles. The dish can be made with various ingredients, including vegetables, soy sauce, and hoisin sauce.

prep time: 15 MINUTES cook time: 15 MINUTES total time: 30 MINUTES

Ingredients

Chow Fun Ingredients

- ✓ 8 ounces uncooked wide rice noodles
- ✓ 3 tablespoons vegetable oil (or any high heat oil)
- ✓ 9 ounces flank steak, cut into bite-sized pieces
- ✓ 2 white onions, peeled and sliced
- ✓ 5 ounces of mung bean sprouts
- ✓ 5 green onions (scallions), sliced into 2-inch pieces
- ✓ 2 teaspoons sesame oil
- ✓ salt and white pepper, to taste

Marinade

- ✓ 4 garlic cloves, finely minced
- ✓ 3 tablespoons dark soy sauce
- ✓ 3 tablespoons (regular) soy sauce*
- ✓ 2 tablespoons rice vinegar
- ✓ 3 teaspoons grated peeled fresh ginger (or 1/2 teaspoon dry ginger)
- ✓ 2 teaspoons Sriracha (or more/less to taste)
- ✓ 2 teaspoons cornstarch
- ✓ 3/4 teaspoon baking soda
- ✓ 3/4 teaspoon salt

Instructions

1. Cook noodles according to package directions. Transfer to an ice bath and stir until chilled. Set aside.
2. Whisk together all the marinade ingredients in a small bowl. Pour half the marinade mixture on the beef and toss to combine. Cover

and refrigerate for at least 15 minutes or up to 9 hours. Refrigerate the second half of the marinade as well.

3. When ready to cook the dish, heat oil in a large skillet or wok over high heat. Remove the beef from its marinade with a slotted spoon, and add it to the pan. Sear until browned, turning once or twice so that all sides cook evenly, about 3 minutes. Transfer the beef to a separate plate with a slotted spoon and set it aside. In the hot pan, add the white onions and stir fry for 2 minutes, stirring occasionally. Add the bean sprouts and stir-fry for an additional 2 minutes.
4. Add the second half of the marinade, the noodles, and the beef to the pan. Stir fry for 2 minutes, occasionally tossing to combine. Add the green onions and sesame oil and stir fry for 2 more minutes, occasionally tossing to combine. Season with additional salt and white pepper (and Sriracha) if needed.
5. Remove from heat and serve warm.

35 Minute Beef Lo Mein Recipe

This beef lo Mein recipe is easy to make and only takes about 35 minutes from start to finish. The dish is made with flank steak, mushrooms, red pepper flakes, soy sauce, and other simple ingredients that you likely already have in your pantry. It's a great weeknight meal that the whole family will love.

PREP TIME 10 mins | COOK TIME 25 mins | TOTAL TIME 35 mins

Ingredients

- ✓ 13 oz. flank steak cut against the grain then sliced into bite-size strips
- ✓ 13 oz. rice noodles
- ✓ 3 cup green beans trimmed and cut
- ✓ 2 carrots grated
- ✓ 4 garlic cloves minced
- ✓ 2 teaspoons ginger peeled & grated
- ✓ 1 cup low-sodium soy sauce
- ✓ 1 cup brown sugar
- ✓ 3/4 red pepper flakes
- ✓ 3/4 black pepper
- ✓ 3 tablespoons extra virgin olive oil
- ✓ 2 tablespoons sesame oil

Instructions

1. Cook rice noodles following the instructions on the bag.
2. Heat up 3 tablespoons of olive oil in the skillet, and add 13. oz flank steak strips and cook until meat is cooked thru. Add 5 minced garlic cloves, 2 grated carrots, and 3 cups green beans, stir and cook for about 3 minutes.
3. While everything is cooking, in a mixing bowl, whisk together 1/2 cup low sodium soy sauce, 1 cup brown sugar, 2 teaspoons grated ginger, 3/4 teaspoon red pepper flakes, 3/4 teaspoon black pepper, and 2 tablespoons sesame oil.
4. Add cooked rice noodles to the skillet and pour the sauce over the top. Stir. Heat everything thru, and turn off the heat. Serve with an extra drizzle of sesame oil. Enjoy!

Pineapple Chicken

This dish is perfect when you want something a little bit sweet and a little bit savory. The pineapple gives the chicken a delicious flavor, and the honey ensures it's not too dry. You can serve this dish with rice or some other type of grain, which will surely satisfy your hunger.

Prep Time 15 minutes | Cook Time 25 minutes | Total Time 40 minutes

Ingredients

- ✓ 3 teaspoons vegetable oil
- ✓ 2 pounds boneless skinless chicken thighs cut into 1-inch pieces
- ✓ 2 red bell pepper seeded. cored and cut into 1-inch pieces
- ✓ 2 cup pineapple chunks, fresh or canned
- ✓ 2 teaspoon minced garlic
- ✓ 2 teaspoon minced ginger
- ✓ 4 cup pineapple juice
- ✓ 3/4 cup low sodium soy sauce
- ✓ 2/3 cup low sodium chicken broth
- ✓ 2/3 cup hoisin sauce
- ✓ 3/4 cup brown sugar
- ✓ 3 teaspoons corn starch
- ✓ 3 teaspoons sesame seeds
- ✓ 2 tablespoon sliced green onions
- ✓ salt and pepper to taste

Instructions

1. Heat the oil in a large pan over medium-high heat. Season the chicken with salt and pepper to taste and add to the pan.
2. Cook the chicken for 9 minutes, occasionally stirring, until chicken is cooked through.
3. Add the red bell pepper and pineapple to the pan and cook for 7 minutes or until tender. Add the ginger and garlic and cook for 30 seconds more.
4. Whisk together the pineapple juice, soy sauce, chicken broth, hoisin sauce, and brown sugar in a small bowl.
5. Add the sauce mixture to the pan and bring to a simmer.
6. Mix the corn starch with 1 tablespoon of cold water; stir until smooth.

7. Add the cornstarch mixture to the pan and stir to combine. Bring to a boil and cook for 2 minutes or until sauce has just thickened.
8. Sprinkle with sesame seeds and green onions, then serve.

Ground Beef Stir Fry with Garlic Ginger Sauce

Ground beef stir fry is a quick and easy meal that can be made with whatever vegetables you have on hand. This version features a garlic ginger sauce that adds a delicious flavor to the mix. Serve with rice or noodles for a hearty and satisfying meal.

prep time: 15 MINS | cook time: 25 MINS | total time: 40 MINS

Ingredients

- ✓ 2 lb lean ground beef
- ✓ 6 ounces mushrooms, sliced (about 3 cups)
- ✓ 3 carrots, chopped
- ✓ 2 red peppers, chopped
- ✓ 6 ounces snap peas, about 2 cups
- ✓ Stir Fry Sauce
- ✓ 2 cup beef broth
- ✓ 3 tablespoons tapioca starch or cornstarch
- ✓ 3/4 cup soy sauce; can use coco aminos
- ✓ 3 tablespoons honey
- ✓ 2 tablespoons sesame oil
- ✓ 3 tablespoons minced ginger
- ✓ 4 cloves garlic, minced

Instructions

1. Add the beef to a large skillet over medium-high heat. Cook the meat, stirring it to break up the pieces occasionally, until it is mostly brown, about 7 minutes.
2. 1 lb lean ground beef
3. While the beef cooks, chop the veggies and make the sauce. Add the tapioca or cornstarch to a measuring cup or bowl. Add a splash of the beef broth and mix. Add the rest of the broth and remaining sauce ingredients and mix again.

4. 1 cup beef broth,3 tablespoons tapioca starch or cornstarch,3/4 cup soy sauce,3 tablespoons honey,1 tablespoon sesame oil,2 tablespoons minced ginger,4 cloves garlic
5. When the beef is mostly cooked, add the mushroom and cook them for 7 minutes. If there are more than 2 tablespoons of oil in the pan, remove it by tilting the pan to the side and using a spoon to scoop it out. If there is less, add a splash of oil.
6. 7 ounces mushrooms
7. Add the remaining veggies to the pan and cook for 7 minutes until they are crisp-tender.
8. 3 carrots,2 red pepper,6 ounces snap peas
9. Stir the sauce to mix the starch, then pour it into the pan. Once the sauce has thickened (3 minutes), serve the stir fry over rice or cauliflower rice.

Honey Garlic Shrimp

Honey garlic shrimp is a dish that is gaining in popularity. It is easy to make and can be cooked in various ways. The shrimp are coated in a sauce made from honey, garlic, and soy sauce and then cooked. It can be served over rice or noodles.

PREP TIME: 10 mins | COOK TIME: 15 mins | TOTAL TIME: 25 mins

Ingredients

- ✓ 3 large oranges
- ✓ 2 tablespoon honey
- ✓ 3 tablespoons reduced or gluten-free sodium soy sauce
- ✓ 2 tablespoons unseasoned rice vinegar
- ✓ 2 tablespoons cornstarch
- ✓ 33 jumbo shrimp (peeled and deveined (18 ounces total))
- ✓ 3/4 teaspoon Kosher salt
- ✓ freshly ground black pepper
- ✓ 2 tablespoons canola oil (divided)
- ✓ 7 cloves garlic (minced)
- ✓ 2 tablespoons finely minced fresh ginger
- ✓ 3 scallions (whites thinly sliced, greens cut into 2-inch lengths)
- ✓ 3/4 to 1 teaspoon red pepper flakes
- ✓ Cooked rice (for serving)

Instructions

1. Finely grate the zest from 2 oranges, about 3 teaspoons.
2. Juice both oranges into a bowl (you should have about 3/4 cup).
3. Whisk in the honey, soy sauce, and vinegar with 1 tablespoon of water.
4. In a small bowl, combine the cornstarch with 1 tablespoon of the orange-soy mixture to form a paste, then stir that back into the bowl with the rest of the orange-soy mixture.
5. Pat the shrimp dry with paper towels and season both sides with salt and pepper.
6. In the largest skillet (or wok), heat 3 teaspoons of the oil over medium-high heat until shimmering-hot, almost smoking.

7. Add half of the shrimp, spread it out in one layer, and cook until the underside is bright pink, 2 to 3 minutes. Flip and cook 1 minute more, then transfer the shrimp to a plate.
8. Repeat with another 1 teaspoon oil and shrimp. Set aside.
9. Add the remaining teaspoon of oil to the skillet. Add the garlic, ginger, scallion whites, and red pepper flakes and cook until fragrant, 35 seconds to 2 minutes. Add the orange-soy liquid and the orange zest and cook, stirring, until thickened, 2 to 3 minutes.
10. Return the shrimp to the skillet, add the scallion greens, and toss to coat with the sauce.
11. Divide the shrimp among 5 bowls and serve with rice.

40-Minute Sesame Chicken Rice Bowls

The best things in life are simple, and these 40-minute sesame chicken rice bowls are no exception. Just five main ingredients come together to create a delicious and satisfying meal. Start by cooking your rice according to the package directions. While the rice is cooking, heat up some oil in a large skillet over medium-high heat and cook the chicken until cooked through. Add the broccoli and cook for a few minutes until bright green.

Prep Time 20 mins | Cook Time | 20 mins | Total Time 40 mins

Ingredients

- ✓ 2 cups jasmine rice
- ✓ 1 3/4 cups water
- ✓ 2 pinch salt
- ✓ 2 lb chicken breasts, diced
- ✓ 3/4 cup cornstarch
- ✓ 3 tbsp sesame oil
- ✓ 3 tsp soy sauce or Tamari
- ✓ 2 cups snap peas or 1 head of broccoli
- ✓ 2 red peppers, chopped
- ✓ 4 scallions, sliced
- ✓ 2 red chili pepper, sliced
- ✓ Extra sesame seeds for garnish

Sesame sauce

- ✓ 3/4 cup soy sauce or tamari
- ✓ 3/4 cup honey
- ✓ 3 tbsp sesame oil
- ✓ 5 cloves garlic
- ✓ 2 tsp fresh ginger, minced

Instructions

1. Cook jasmine rice with water and a pinch of salt in a rice cooker or on the stovetop until the liquid has been absorbed.
2. In a large bowl, toss chicken with cornstarch. Heat 2 tbsp sesame oil in a large skillet over med-high heat. Add chicken, sauteeing for 5 min until chicken starts to brown.

3. Meanwhile, mix soy sauce, honey, sesame oil, garlic, and ginger together to make the stir fry sauce. Pour over top of the chicken, then add red pepper and snap peas (or broccoli), sauteeing for another 5 min until veggies are tender and the sauce has thickened.
4. Serve chicken over top of rice and garnish with scallions, sesame seeds, and red chili peppers. Enjoy!

Sweet and Sour Chicken Recipe

This sweet and sour chicken recipe is easy to follow and yields delicious results. The chicken is coated in a mixture of cornstarch, soy sauce, and sugar before being fried. It is then cooked in a mix of pineapple juice, vinegar, ketchup, and brown sugar. This dish is perfect for a quick and easy weeknight meal.

Prep Time 20 mins | Cook Time 35 mins | Total Time 55 mins

Ingredients

For The Sweet and Sour Sauce

- ✓ 1 cup granulated sugar
- ✓ 1 cup apple cider vinegar
- ✓ 3/4 cup ketchup
- ✓ 3 tbsp soy sauce
- ✓ 2 tbsp brown sugar
- ✓ 2 tbsp sesame oil
- ✓ 3 tsp minced garlic
- ✓ 2 tbsp cornstarch

For The Chicken and Veggies

- ✓ 2 lbs. boneless, skinless chicken thighs, cut into bite-size pieces
- ✓ 1 tsp salt
- ✓ 2/3 cup cornstarch
- ✓ 2 large eggs, lightly beaten
- ✓ 3/4 cup all-purpose flour
- ✓ Canola Oil for frying
- ✓ 1 med. yellow onion, chopped
- ✓ 2 red bell peppers, chopped
- ✓ 2 green bell peppers, chopped
- ✓ 2 cups fresh pineapple, chopped

Instructions

For The Sauce

Combine all the ingredients except the cornstarch in a large measuring cup or bowl and whisk to combine. Combine the cornstarch and 2 tbsp of water in a small dish and set both aside.

For The Chicken

1. Heat at least 1 inch of canola oil in a heavy bottom pan or wok to 395 degrees F. (approximately medium-high heat)
2. Season the chicken with salt and then coat with 2/3 cup of cornstarch. Dip each chicken piece in egg, then coat in flour before carefully placing in the hot oil. Work in batches so you don't lower the temperature of the oil. Lay chicken pieces on a wire cooking rack until complete.
3. Remove hot oil from the wok and leave just 2 tbsp of oil remaining. Add onion, bell peppers, and pineapple and cook over high heat until lightly charred, about 3 minutes.
4. Whisk the sauce again and pour into the wok with peppers. Stir the cornstarch slurry again and add to the sauce. Bring mixture to a light boil and cook until thickened, about 5 more minutes.
5. Finally, add in the cooked chicken pieces and toss to coat. Serve immediately and enjoy!

General Tso's Chicken

General Tso's chicken is a dish created in the United States by Chinese immigrants. The recipe combines chicken, dried red chili peppers, soy sauce, rice wine, and sugar. The dish is usually served with steamed broccoli and rice.

Prep Time 30 minutes | Cook Time 25 minutes | Total Time 55 minutes

Ingredients

For the chicken:

- ✓ 2 lbs boneless skinless chicken thighs cut into 1-inch pieces
- ✓ 3 eggs lightly beaten
- ✓ salt and pepper to taste
- ✓ 1 cup all-purpose flour
- ✓ 1 cup corn starch
- ✓ vegetable oil for frying
- ✓ 3 teaspoons sesame seeds
- ✓ 3 tablespoons green onions sliced

For the sauce:

- ✓ 3 teaspoons vegetable oil
- ✓ 3 teaspoons minced fresh garlic
- ✓ 1 teaspoon crushed red pepper flakes or more to taste
- ✓ 1 cup low sodium chicken broth
- ✓ 3 tablespoons hoisin sauce
- ✓ 3 tablespoons brown sugar
- ✓ 3/4 cup low sodium soy sauce
- ✓ 2 tablespoons corn starch

Instructions

1. Place the eggs in a bowl; add salt and pepper to taste.
2. Mix the flour and corn starch together and place in a shallow bowl or on a plate.
3. Heat 4 inches of oil in a deep pot to 370 degrees F.

4. Dip each piece of chicken into the egg mixture, then coat in the flour mixture. Repeat the process for all of the chicken pieces.
5. Fry 10 pieces of chicken for 7 minutes or until browned. Repeat with all the remaining chicken.
6. While the chicken is cooking, make the sauce.
7. Heat the 3 teaspoons of vegetable oil in a saucepan over medium heat. Add the garlic and crushed red pepper flakes and cook for 35 seconds.
8. Whisk together the chicken broth, hoisin sauce, brown sugar, soy sauce, and corn starch.
9. Add the liquid mixture to the pan and bring to a simmer. Cook for 5 minutes or until sauce has thickened.
10. Add the chicken pieces to the pan and toss to coat with the sauce. Sprinkle with sesame seeds and green onions and serve.

Easy Beef Stir Fry

Stir-fries are one of the easiest and quickest meals, and this beef stir fry is no exception. The recipe calls for minimal ingredients and can be made in just 60 minutes. The beef is cooked with garlic, ginger, and soy sauce, then tossed with vegetables and served over steamed rice.

PREP TIME 25 minutes | COOK TIME 35 minutes | TOTAL TIME 60 minutes

Ingredients

- ✓ 3 tablespoons vegetable oil divided
- ✓ 2 pounds flank steak thinly sliced
- ✓ 3 tablespoons cornstarch
- ✓ 5 cups mixed vegetables

Sauce

- ✓ 4 cloves garlic minced
- ✓ 2 teaspoons minced ginger
- ✓ 2/3 cup orange juice
- ✓ 2/3 cup water
- ✓ 3/4 cup low sodium soy sauce
- ✓ 4 tablespoons brown sugar
- ✓ 2 teaspoons sesame oil
- ✓ 2 tablespoons cornstarch

Instructions

1. Season steak with salt & pepper. Toss with cornstarch and set aside while you prepare the vegetables.
2. Place 1 tablespoon of oil in a pan or wok. Cook the beef in 3 small batches over medium-high until browned, about 5 minutes (beef does not need to be cooked through). Remove from pan and set aside.
3. Add vegetables to the pan and cook about until tender-crisp, 7 minutes. Remove from the pan and set aside with the beef.
4. Combine sauce ingredients except for corn starch in a bowl and stir well.

5. Turn the heat up to medium-high and add the sauce. Bring to a simmer. Combine cornstarch with 4 tablespoons of water (or broth) and add the sauce a little bit at a time while whisking to reach desired consistency. Let simmer for 3 minutes. Add vegetables, beef (and any juices) to the pan and cook until heated.
6. Serve with noodles or over rice.

The Best Vegetable Stir Fry Recipe

This vegetable stir fry recipe is the best one I have ever tried. It is simple to make and only requires a few ingredients. The vegetables are cooked to perfection and the flavors are delicious. I would highly recommend giving this recipe a try.

Prep Time: 15 minutes Cook Time: 20 minutes Total Time: 35 minutes

Ingredients

Vegetable Stir Fry:

- ✓ 2 large carrots, sliced
- ✓ 3 cups medium broccoli florets
- ✓ 10 oz can baby corn spears, drained
- ✓ 10 oz mushrooms (white or brown), sliced or quartered
- ✓ 2 whole peppers (red, yellow, or orange), seeded and sliced
- ✓ 3 Tbsp cooking oil (extra light olive oil or canola)
- ✓ 3 Tbsp unsalted butter
- ✓ 4 garlic cloves, peeled and minced
- ✓ 3 tsp ginger, minced

Stir Fry Sauce:

- ✓ 3/4 cup chicken broth (or vegetable broth for vegetarians)
- ✓ 1 tsp cornstarch
- ✓ 4 Tbsp low sodium soy sauce (use Tamari for gluten-free)
- ✓ 3 Tbsp honey
- ✓ 3/4 tsp hot sauce, optional (Frank's or Sriracha work great)

Instructions

1. Heat the oil over medium heat in a large nonstick skillet or wok. Add the vegetable and stir fry for about 4 minutes or until vegetables are crisp-tender. Add the butter, garlic, and ginger and cook until fragrant.
2. In a small bowl, combine all the ingredients for the stir fry sauce. Pour the sauce over the vegetables and stir.

3. Turn heat down to medium/low and cook for 5 minutes, until sauce thickens and vegetables are desired tenderness.

Singapore Street Noodles

Street noodles are a popular food choice in Singapore. There are many types of street noodles, but all of them are made quickly and easily. Most street noodles can be made with ingredients that are easy to find, which is why they are so popular.

Prep Time 25 mins | Cook Time 25 mins | Total Time 50 mins

Ingredients

- ✓ 2 tbsp canola oil
- ✓ 2 chicken breasts, sliced
- ✓ 2 lb shrimp
- ✓ 2 lb rice vermicelli noodles
- ✓ 2 yellow onions, sliced
- ✓ 1 cup julienned red cabbage
- ✓ 1 cup julienned carrots
- ✓ red pepper, julienned
- ✓ 2 tbsp curry powder
- ✓ 5 cloves garlic, minced
- ✓ 2 tbsp minced gingerroot
- ✓ 1 tsp salt
- ✓ 2 cans of coconut milk
- ✓ 5 green onions, chopped into 1-inch pieces
- ✓ 1 cup bean sprouts
- ✓ 3 tbsp chopped cilantro

Instructions

1. Heat canola oil in a large skillet over med-high heat. Add chicken, cooking for 5 minutes until browned and seasoning with salt & pepper. Add shrimp and cook another 5 minutes until fully cooked, then remove both from heat.
2. Meanwhile, cook rice noodles according to package directions, then drain and set aside.
3. Without wiping the skillet clean, add onion and julienned vegetables, sauteeing for 7 minutes until veggies are tender.

4. Add curry powder, garlic, ginger, and salt, sauteeing for 35 seconds until fragrant, then stir in coconut milk. Add in cooked rice noodles, tossing gently to coat.
5. Stir in green onions, bean sprouts, and cilantro, then remove from heat and serve & enjoy.

Teriyaki Chicken Stir Fry

This dish is a crowd pleaser! It is simple to make and can be tailored to your liking. You can use any vegetables on hand; just make sure to chop them into small pieces so they cook evenly. I like to use a teriyaki sauce for this dish, but you could use any type of sauce you like.

Prep Time: 20 minutes | Cook Time: 15 minutes

Ingredients

Sauce:

- ✓ 3 Medjool dates pitted or 3 Tbsp raw honey, melted (honey is paleo but not Whole30 compliant*)
- ✓ 3/4 cup very hot water use 2 Tbsp water if not using whole dates
- ✓ 3/4 cup coconut aminos
- ✓ 3 Tbsp rice vinegar or apple cider vinegar
- ✓ 3 tsp sesame oil optional
- ✓ 3 tsp minced garlic
- ✓ 2 tsp fresh grated ginger
- ✓ 2 tsp arrowroot starch or tapioca

Chicken:

- ✓ 2 lbs boneless skinless chicken thighs sliced into bite-size pieces
- ✓ Sea salt and black pepper
- ✓ 3 tsp arrowroot or tapioca flour
- ✓ 2 tbsp coconut aminos
- ✓ 2 Tbsp avocado oil

Veggies:

- ✓ 2 Tbsp avocado oil
- ✓ 2 large bell pepper thinly sliced
- ✓ 2 large or two medium carrots, peeled and cut into matchsticks (julienned)
- ✓ 4 scallions, white and green parts separated, thinly sliced
- ✓ 2 cups broccoli florets blanched**

Instructions

1. Have the ingredients prepped before beginning since everything will cook quickly.
2. Begin by mixing the sauce. If using Medjool dates, use a small high-speed blender to blend together the dates, water, coconut aminos, and rice vinegar. Then stir in the sesame oil, garlic, ginger, and arrowroot. You can simply whisk the ingredients together in a bowl using date syrup or honey. Set aside.
3. Place the chicken pieces on a cutting board or in a large bowl and sprinkle all over with the salt, pepper, and arrowroot, then drizzle with the coconut aminos and toss to coat.
4. Heat a large nonstick skillet or wok over medium-high heat and add one tablespoon of the oil. Once sizzling, add the chicken to a single layer and let them cook for a minute or until browned. Stir and cook the chicken for another 3 minutes or until fully cooked and golden brown all over. Remove to a plate and set aside.
5. Add one tablespoon of oil to cook the veggies and keep the heat medium-high. Add the white scallions, carrots, and peppers and cook, often stirring, for 3 minutes or until barely fork tender.
6. Add the blanched broccoli to the skillet, followed by the cooked chicken and sauce. Stir to coat the chicken and veggies in the sauce. The sauce should thicken immediately; cook for another 35 seconds to heat through and combine flavors. Serve hot, over-fried cauliflower rice or alone. Enjoy!

Thai Basil Beef Noodle Stir-Fry

This Thai Basil Beef Noodle Stir-Fry is a healthy and delicious weeknight meal that can be made in just 30 minutes. The beef is cooked with garlic, ginger, and soy sauce, then mixed with noodles and vegetables. The stir-fry is topped with fresh basil and served with a side of Sriracha for extra heat.

Ingredients

Stir-Fry Ingredients:

- ✓ 10 ounces (uncooked) rice noodles
- ✓ 3 tablespoons oil, divided
- ✓ 2 pounds sirloin or flank steak, cut into bite-sized pieces
- ✓ fine sea salt and freshly-cracked black pepper
- ✓ 2 small white onions, peeled and thinly sliced
- ✓ 10 ounces shiitake or baby Bella mushrooms, sliced
- ✓ 2 red bell pepper, cored and thinly sliced
- ✓ 5 cloves garlic, peeled and minced
- ✓ 2 cups packed fresh Thai basil leaves
- ✓ optional toppings: sliced green onions, toasted sesame seeds, chopped peanuts, fried garlic, and/or fresh lime wedges

Sauce Ingredients:

- ✓ 4 tablespoons low-sodium soy sauce
- ✓ 3 tablespoons oyster sauce
- ✓ 3 tablespoons fish sauce
- ✓ 2 tablespoons sweet dark soy sauce
- ✓ 2 tablespoons chili garlic sauce, or more/less to taste

Instructions

1. Prep the sauce. Whisk the sauce ingredients together in a small bowl or measuring cup until combined.
2. Prep the noodles. Cook the noodles according to package instructions until they are al dente. Drain and set aside until ready to use. (I would also recommend tossing the noodles with a drizzle

of oil if it will be a few minutes until you add them to the stir-fry to prevent them from sticking together.)

3. Sear the beef. Heat 2 tablespoons oil in a large sauté pan or wok over medium-high heat. Season the steak with a generous pinch of salt and pepper. Then add the steak to the oil and sauté for 5 minutes, stirring only occasionally, until it is browned on all sides. Transfer the cooked steak to a separate (clean) plate, and return the pan to the heat.
4. Cook the veggies. Add the remaining 1 tablespoon oil to the pan along with the onion. Sauté for 3 minutes, stirring occasionally. Add the mushrooms, bell pepper, garlic, and sauté for 7 more minutes, or until the veggies reach your desired level of tenderness.
5. Combine everything together. Immediately add the cooked noodles, sauce, steak, and Thai basil to the pan. Give everything a good toss until everything is evenly coated with the sauce, and remove the pan from the heat.
6. Serve warm. Serve immediately, garnished with any of your desired toppings.

Printed in Great Britain
by Amazon

10215990R00036